JULIAN ASSANGE

Essential Lives

JULIAN ASSANGE

WIKILEAKS FOUNDER

by **Melissa Higgins**

Content Consultant:
Nora Paul, director
Minnesota Journalism Center, University of Minnesota

ABDO
Publishing Company

CREDITS

Published by ABDO Publishing Company, 8000 West 78th Street, Edina, Minnesota 55439. Copyright © 2012 by Abdo Consulting Group, Inc. International copyrights reserved in all countries. No part of this book may be reproduced in any form without written permission from the publisher. The Essential Library™ is a trademark and logo of ABDO Publishing Company.

Printed in the United States of America,
North Mankato, Minnesota
062011
092011

♻ THIS BOOK CONTAINS AT LEAST 10% RECYCLED MATERIALS.

Editor: Mari Kesselring
Copy Editor: Rebecca Rowell
Cover Design: Kazuko Collins
Interior Design and Production: Marie Tupy

Library of Congress Cataloging-in-Publication Data
Higgins, Melissa, 1953-
  Julian Assange : WikiLeaks founder / by Melissa Higgins.
    p. cm. -- (Essential lives)
  Includes bibliographical references and index.
  ISBN 978-1-61783-001-3
  1. Assange, Julian--Juvenile literature. 2. WikiLeaks (Organization)--Juvenile literature. 3. Editors--Australia--Biography--Juvenile literature. 4. Publishers and publishing--Biography--Juvenile literature. 5. Radicals--Biography--Juvenile literature. 6. Leaks (Disclosure of information)--Political aspects--Juvenile literature. 7. Official secrets--Juvenile literature. 8. Whistle blowing--Political aspects--Juvenile literature. I. Title.
  PN5516.A87H54 2012
  070.92--dc22
  [B]
                                                    2011010075

TABLE OF CONTENTS

Julian Assange is the founder of WikiLeaks, a Web-based organization that publishes classified documents and information.

The Most Dangerous Man

*I*n late March and early April 2010, Julian Assange was holed up in a small house in Reykjavík, Iceland. He and his associates called it the Bunker. Keeping the curtains closed at all times, Assange had filled the house's stark rooms with

computers and a group of dedicated
volunteers. They were working
around the clock on what Assange
called Project B. They were getting
a highly classified US military video
ready to release to the world.

Within a week, Assange and his staff
would finish decrypting, analyzing,
and editing the raw video. They
would create a media campaign to
go with its release. And they would
strengthen computer security to make
sure the video would be impossible to remove from
the Internet once it was posted. Assange would even
send two investigators to Baghdad, Iraq, to gather
information on the incident portrayed in the video.

For Assange, the hidden location and closed
drapes were necessary. Assange knew he was being
watched. The Icelandic police had taken photographs
of him. And he suspected he was being followed. He
had been under law-enforcement scrutiny for years,
having made enemies first by his computer hacking,
and now with his Web site—WikiLeaks. WikiLeaks
is a Web site and media organization that publishes
classified material and information.

Robin Hood of Hacking

"Robin Hood of Hacking"
was how *The Irish Times*
titled a June 2010 article
on Assange. The article
explains, "With his halo
of martyrdom, shield of
truth and righteous sword
at the ready to slay the
beasts of government lies
and military cover-ups,
the Australian journalist
Julian Assange . . . is like
some freedom-of-infor-
mation cartoon hero
come to life."[1]

WikiLeaks's Web site posts leaks.
It also serves as a digital drop box for leaked information.

Collateral Murder

Since going public with WikiLeaks in December 2006, the negative attention on Assange had increased. He had received more than 100 threats because of the material posted on the Web site. The US military would definitely not be pleased with WikiLeaks's next release—an 18-minute video Assange titled *Collateral Murder*.

Collateral Murder plays out a disturbing scene. From the cockpit of an Apache helicopter, the video shows at least 12 people being killed by US soldiers in Baghdad, Iraq, on July 12, 2007. Among the casualties were two journalists from the Reuters news agency. Two children were also seriously injured. On the audio track, the helicopter pilots can be heard mocking the dead. The pilots are seemingly aware they are shooting civilians. The chilling scenes and audio countered the US Army's official record of the incident: except for the journalists, only insurgents were killed.

By releasing the video, Assange wanted to prove that the army was covering up the truth. He also wanted to show that media coverage of military operations could not be trusted, especially when it came to reporting who was—and who was not— an insurgent. Ultimately, Assange hoped to sway public opinion against the wars in Iraq and Afghanistan. Assange considered the wars illegal and immoral.

"Playing Video Games with People's Lives"

In a televised interview on MSNBC, Assange said that *Collateral Murder* "shows the debasement and moral corruption of soldiers as a result of war. It seems like they are playing video games with people's lives."[2] In an interview on Russian Television, Assange added, "The problem is not just a few stray pilots. This is a systemic problem at the company level and in the rules of engagement."[3]

In the Bunker, Assange and his group barely finished their task with enough time for Assange to throw his clothes, computer hard drives, and several cell phones into a worn backpack. He raced to catch his flight to Washington DC. He arrived there on April 5, 2010, at 2:00 a.m. A few hours later, he appeared at the National Press Club where he played *Collateral Murder* for the crowd of journalists in attendance.

The video was posted on WikiLeaks and on YouTube. What was once a fringe Web site with a largely mysterious founder had now gone mainstream.

Reaction

By April 6, 2010, *Collateral Murder* had been viewed more than 2 million times on YouTube. Television news reports replayed it hundreds of times. Assange gave several interviews and the story was covered in newspapers, magazines, and television programs around the world.

At first, the United States was widely criticized for the actions of its military personnel in Iraq. Iraqi journalists and politicians were outraged. Those who valued government transparency praised Assange and WikiLeaks.

The Reuters news agency expressed amazement over what Assange had done. For more than two years, the organization had tried to gain access to the raw video from the Pentagon through the Freedom of Information Act but was always denied. Experts wondered how Assange was able to get this classified video outside of normal channels. He refused to reveal his source. The Pentagon put Assange on its watch list.

Meanwhile, the US military offered a different viewpoint of the events captured in *Collateral Murder*. US Defense Secretary Robert Gates said the footage was taken out of context from the events that happened before and after it. The military insisted that people on the ground were carrying weapons, and the rules of engagement had been correctly followed. As the days passed, the media began to shift its focus away

The Rules of Engagement Were Followed

The US military conducted an investigation into the Baghdad helicopter attack shown in *Collateral Murder* and concluded US troops acted appropriately. The US military claimed the people on the ground were carrying weapons, while others claimed the pilots just saw cameras the reporters were carrying. Even if the pilots had seen cameras, it was not uncommon for insurgent groups to photograph US military and their own activity for use in training videos and in propaganda. The reporters were intermixed among the insurgents and therefore difficult to distinguish. Additionally, the attack happened right after security forces had come under fire and insurgents were known to be in the area.

from Assange's point of view. News commentators and analysts started agreeing with the military's version of events. Many believed the pilots had probably mistaken the newsman's camera as a rocket-propelled grenade. Whether in his favor or not, the publicity increased the aura of mystery surrounding Assange.

Who Is Julian Assange?

Not much was known about the man from WikiLeaks. Assange did not do many interviews, nor did he like talking about himself. The few photographs and video footage that existed of him showed a tall, thin man, with gray eyes and a heap of silver-white hair. He spoke slowly and softly. It was known that he was originally from Australia and that he had lived in various parts of the world, including Iceland, Sweden, and Africa.

In their scramble to learn more, many reporters started with the WikiLeaks Web site. In one magazine article, a journalist explained, "Designed as a digital drop box, the site is a place where anyone can anonymously post sensitive information."[4] Its advocates said WikiLeaks was a Web site where confidential information could be safely released.

While WikiLeaks had gotten some publicity prior to the Iraq video release on April 5, 2010, Assange had never made a public announcement related to any post. Buzz about documents released on WikiLeaks was mostly generated by word of mouth. Now, this private man on a quest to expose injustice was in a very bright spotlight.

In a television interview, Assange explained why he chose to go public with the Iraq video:

> *This is an attack on one of our own. This is an attack on journalists trying to get the truth out, so I suppose we have felt an extra camaraderie and a need to defend ourselves and our community by exposing the attack on these journalists in Iraq.*[5]

WikiLeaks Scoops before April 2010

According to the WikiLeaks Web site, "Wikileaks has released more classified intelligence documents than the rest of the world combined."[6] Prior to the April 2010 posting of *Collateral Murder*, some of WikiLeaks's most newsworthy scoops included:

- Memos about the dumping of toxic material off the African coast
- Sarah Palin's private e-mails
- The US Army's Guantanamo Bay prison camp operating procedures
- E-mails in which scientists discuss manipulating climate-change data
- An Australian Internet blacklist
- Names and addresses of the members of the far-right British National Party
- 500,000 messages sent on the day of the September 11 attacks in New York City
- A British military manual with directions on how to avoid leaks

Even with the increased attention, Assange was not close to being finished with revealing secret documents through WikiLeaks. He was preparing in the coming days to post a second classified military video—this one showing a US air attack in Afghanistan, again killing civilians.

By striking blows at institutions as powerful as the US military, Assange was being hailed as the Robin Hood of hacking and the James Bond of journalism. But within a few months, he would also earn a more sinister title: the most dangerous man in the world.

"Every organization rests upon a mountain of secrets."[7]

—*Assange*

The son of Saeed Chmagh, a Reuters driver killed in the incident shown in Collateral Murder, holds up an image of his father.

*Julian was born in Townsville, Australia,
but he would move often throughout his childhood.*

A Vagabond Boyhood
in Australia

As reporters dug into the background of the mysterious newsmaker, it became apparent that Assange had been living a nomadic life. He moved frequently from place to place and country to country, carrying his few possessions in a backpack. Assange's rootless lifestyle began at an early age.

Julian was born on July 3, 1971, in Townsville, on the northeast coast of Queensland, Australia. His mother's family came to Australia from Scotland in the mid-1800s. Soon after Julian's birth his parents were no longer a couple, and Julian had no contact with his biological father, John Shipton. In fact, he got his last name from his stepfather, Brett Assange, who his mother married when Julian was one year old.

Julian moved often with his mother, Christine Hawkins, and Brett. Julian's parents operated a small theater company. Brett directed the plays, and Christine made the sets. The family lived for a while near Townsville on Magnetic Island, which had about 500 residents at the time. Young Julian fished, had a horse, built a raft, and explored mine shafts. He told an interviewer, "Most of this period of my childhood was pretty Tom Sawyer."[1] However, the house on Magnetic Island burned to the ground in an accidental fire.

It is unclear where the family lived after their house was destroyed. But, when Julian was eight, his mother

"We were bright sensitive kids who didn't fit into the dominant subculture and fiercely castigated those who did as irredeemable boneheads."[2]

—Assange

left Brett. She began a relationship with an amateur musician, Keith Hamilton. When Julian was nine, his mother divorced Brett. Christine and Keith had a son together, giving Julian a half brother. But the rocky relationship did not last long. Keith was manipulative and abusive. Christine worried that he wanted to take her second son. Julian, his new half brother, and Christine went on the run.

Julian ran and hid with his mother and half brother across the country for five years, from the age of 11 until he was 16. He moved 37 times by the time he was 14.

EARLY EDUCATION

Julian attended at least 12 schools, never for more than a few months at a time. He was mostly homeschooled by his mother, due partly to their frequent moves, but also because Christine distrusted authority. When Christine was 17 years old, she had burned her schoolbooks and ran away from home on a motorcycle. She thought her children's curiosity and spirits would be broken by the formal education system.

In addition to being homeschooled, Julian took correspondence courses and read on his own, especially science. He would spend hours poring over books in libraries, often reading lists of citations and then studying the author's sources. He sometimes studied with college professors. Soon, Julian became interested in a new technology—personal computing.

A Passion for Hacking

When Julian was 13, his mother rented a house across the street from an electronics store. There, Julian fell in love with an early personal computer, a Commodore 64. He would play with and write programs for the computer while in the store. His mother saved her money and bought him the computer for $600. "Julian had been drooling over these things [computers] for about a year and I just thought that he really needed to

An Early Mistrust of Authority

When Julian was a child, his mother helped activists gather information about nuclear tests being conducted in the Australian outback. Late one night, with her son in the car, police stopped them on the road and told Christine she should stay out of politics. They said dealing in politics might make it appear that she was an unfit mother. As a result of the threatening encounter, Christine stayed out of politics for the next ten years to protect Julian. According to Julian, it was one of his earliest examples of abuse of power and secrecy.

have it for his intellectual growth," Christine said in an interview. "I was just indulging his childhood passion."[5]

Julian broke into the computer's software, just to see if he could. Surprisingly, he found hidden messages left there by the software's programmers. Thus, began his obsession with the hidden world of computing. Julian compared the challenge of working with computers to playing chess. The computer became a substitute for the friends Julian had difficulty making due to his frequent moves. Even his mother recognized that the computer had become somewhat of an addiction for him.

In 1987, at age 16, Julian got his first computer modem. Although Web sites were not in use, corporate and government computers had linked networks that could be broken into, or hacked. This is exactly what Julian and two of his friends did. They hacked into highly secure networks,

"What has happened is that as a young boy traveling from state to state and school to school and from country town to country town his mother purchased a computer for him . . . that computer, in effect, became his only friend and his only interaction with the outside world."[6]

—Paul Galbally, Julian's attorney, to the Victorian County Court, 1996

including the US Department of Defense and the Los Alamos Laboratory in New Mexico. Julian and his friends called themselves the International Subversives. Using the pseudonym Mendax, which is from the ancient Roman philosopher Horace and means "nobly untruthful," Julian seemed comfortable with his outsider status.

Julian was gaining a reputation as a skilled programmer and hacker. But, he was also getting attention from law enforcement. Accused of stealing money from CitiBank, the state police raided his

What Is Hacking?

Hacking is when a person accesses someone else's computer without permission. Some people hack for fun. They get into systems just to see if they can, or to learn from the information they find. Other "white hat" hackers are computer security professionals who use their awareness of computer weaknesses to come up with new protections. There is also a darker side to hacking. Corporate "black hat" hackers access rival companies' computers to steal competitors' information. A government might spy on another government by hacking into its computers. A hacker might try to knock out a city's energy grid or a government's military network by placing malicious code into a software program.

Some people use hacking as a form of political activism, called "hacktivism." Accessing information that is locked away from public view, "hacktivists" hope to reveal government behavior so embarrassing—and possibly illegal—that the resulting public alarm will bring about change. Whether hacking is done for fun, for political activism, or for other reasons, breaking into a private or public computer network is illegal in the United States and most other countries.

house. They took his computer equipment. Julian was not charged with any crime and his equipment was returned. This was Julian's first experience getting into legal trouble with his hacking habit.

LOVE AND MARRIAGE LOST

When Julian was 18, he fell in love with a 16-year-old girl he met through a mutual friend. He briefly moved in with her. It was a few days later that his computer equipment was taken by state police. Hoping to get away from the law, the couple moved to Melbourne after his equipment was returned. But Julian found out his girlfriend was pregnant, so the couple moved back to be closer to Julian's mother.

Julian and his girlfriend married in 1989, when he was 18 and she was 17. A few months later, their son, Daniel, was born. The marriage lasted only a short time, and his wife left with the baby. It was a dark period in Julian's life. Upset over losing his wife and son, and worried about being arrested, he was not eating or sleeping much.

But regardless of the trouble he could get into, Julian did not stop hacking. It was a reassuring constant in his life. Hacking gave him a sense of accomplishment. ⌐

From a young age, Julian enjoyed hacking.

Assange and the International Subversives hacked into Nortel's computer systems.

LEGAL BATTLES

With each hacking success, Assange became bolder. He left messages for network administrators of the computer systems he hacked into, bragging about his skill. In 1991, when he turned 20, he and his friends in the

International Subversives began a new project. They were hacking into the main Melbourne terminal of the Canadian telecom giant, Nortel.

Soon Assange realized law enforcement was monitoring the trio's activities. The police named their investigation Operation Weather. In return, Assange began tapping the telephones of the people watching him. He became more nervous. He was so afraid of being raided by the police that he kept his computer disks hidden near beehives.

Assange hacked into the Nortel computer at odd hours, when it was mostly inactive. But one night, a Nortel administrator was logged in at the same time as Assange. Trying to defuse the situation, Assange wrote the administrator a few lighthearted notes. For example, "It's been nice playing with your system. We didn't do any damage and we even improved a few things. Please don't call the Australian Federal Police."[1]

Assange's Golden Rules of Hacking

In the book he cowrote with Suelette Dreyfus, *Underground: Tales of Hacking, Madness, and Obsession on the Electronic Frontier*, Assange laid out his golden rules of hacker subculture: "Don't damage computer systems you break into (including crashing them); don't change the information in those systems (except for altering logs to cover your tracks); and share information."[2]

HACKING BATTLE

But Nortel did claim the hacking had caused damage to its computer systems. The company said it would cost more than $100,000 to repair. The Melbourne police arrested Assange in 1991. He was charged with 31 counts of hacking and other related crimes. It would take three more years before the case would come to trial. Prosecutors wanted to make sure they had a solid case. It was the first Australian case of its kind. Prosecutors hoped it would discourage other hackers.

During those three years, Assange briefly stayed with his mom. Then, he took to sleeping outside in a eucalyptus forest. Although the mosquitoes were so bad their bites would scar his face, he found that living outside by himself quieted his mind. At one point, he became so depressed he checked himself into a hospital for a few days.

Awaiting his trial, Assange also stopped hacking and began working as a computer software developer. In 1993, he helped establish Suburbia Public Access Network. It was one of the first Internet service providers (ISPs) in Australia. It became popular with activist groups and organizations concerned with issues of free speech.

"People were fleeing from ISPs that would fold under legal threats," Assange told an interviewer. He continued,

> *That's something I saw early on, without realizing it: potentiating people to reveal their information, creating a [channel]. Without having any other robust publisher in the market, people came to us.*[3]

By the time the Nortel case went to trial in 1994, the other members of the International Subversives had decided to work with investigators. But Assange was convinced he had done nothing wrong. He believed his hacking had harmed no one. Regardless of what Nortel claimed,

The Nortel Case: Criminal Activity or Innocent Mischief?

The lead lawyer for the prosecution in the 1991 Nortel case admitted that Assange was not a malicious hacker. "The information retrieved was not used for personal gain. . . . The motive behind the hacking was simply an arrogance and a desire to show off computer skill." He added, "[Assange] is clearly a person who wants the internet to be able to provide material to people that isn't paid for."[4] Ken Day, who led Australia's federal investigation into the Nortel case, said of Assange,

> He was opposed to Big Brother, to the restriction of freedom of communication. His moral sense about breaking into computer systems was, "I'm not going to do any harm, so what's wrong with it?"[5]

The judge in the case did not seem too upset with the crimes, blaming them on Assange's smart and inquisitive nature. Of Assange's tapping police telephones, the judge said, "If I may say so, [Assange] seemed to be one jump ahead of everybody."[6]

he did not think any damage had been done to the company's computers. He decided to fight the charges. He also kept busy with other work. In 1995, Assange cowrote Strobe, a free open-source port-scanner program which automatically scans and tests all the communication ports of a system looking for open ports.

Some counts against Assange in the Nortel case were eventually dropped. He changed his mind about fighting the charges. Assange pleaded guilty on December 5, 1996. Although he faced a potential ten-year prison sentence, the judge seemed to agree with Assange's argument that it was a victimless crime. At the sentencing, the judge said,

> There is just no evidence that there was anything other than sort of intelligent inquisitiveness and the pleasure of being able to—what's the expression—surf through these various computers.[7]

Assange was sentenced to three years of probation and had to pay a $2,300 fine.

Assange continued to work with computer programs. Around 1997, he cocreated Rubberhose. Rubberhose was an encryption program to help protect the sensitive computer data of journalists and human-rights workers. Assange also worked with author Suelette Dreyfus on the book *Underground: Tales of Hacking, Madness, and Obsession on the Electronic Frontier*. It was published in 1997. The book features a character named Mendax, whose activities closely reflected Assange's own life.

BATTLE FOR HIS SON

As the Nortel case was proceeding, Assange tried to gain full custody of his son, who was now about five years old, from his ex-wife. Assange believed his ex-wife and her new boyfriend posed a risk to Daniel. But the state's child-protection agency did not agree. A lengthy and bitter battle followed.

Experiencing what they believed was wrongdoing by the Australian child-protection agency, Assange, his mother, and another activist created Parent Inquiry Into Child Protection. Through this

Encryption

Encryption software changes computer data into a secret code so that it can be transmitted securely. Encryption is especially important for human-rights workers and journalists who need to maintain sensitive information in the field, such as names of activists or details of abuse incidents. For example, if a human-rights worker carrying a laptop loaded with confidential names were stopped on a road by an armed military patrol, it would not be difficult for the patrol to get the worker's computer password through torture. They would then have easy access to the data on the computer, which could put many lives at risk. If encrypted, however, the sensitive data could not be read.

organization, they built a database of legal records on child custody cases. Child-protection workers provided the information for the database. Assange's organization gave the workers an anonymous place to share what they knew. After many legal hearings and appeals, Assange finally worked out a custody agreement with his ex-wife in 1999.

Life after Hacking

That same year, Assange registered the Web domain name leaks.org. He never did anything with the site, but it hinted at his early interest in a project like WikiLeaks. When the custody battle for his son ended, Assange helped support Daniel with various paying jobs. He turned his hacking knowledge into work as a computer-security consultant.

Hoping to find the same mental challenge he got from hacking with college courses, Assange studied

No Longer Hacking

Assange dislikes when people still refer to him as a computer hacker. He told a magazine interviewer, "Because I co-wrote a book about [being a hacker], there are documentaries about that, people talk about that a lot. . . . But that was 20 years ago. It's very annoying to see modern day articles calling me a computer hacker. I'm not ashamed of it, I'm quite proud of it. But I understand the reason they suggest I'm a computer hacker now. . . . It's done quite deliberately by some of our opponents."[8]

mathematics and physics at the University of Melbourne beginning in 2003. But, he felt stifled by the school's hierarchy and desire for conformity. He also became convinced that individuals at the university were sharing their work with the military. This bothered Assange a great deal. He left the university in 2006 without completing his degree.

An Emerging Philosophy

A distrust of authority had become a repeating theme in Assange's life. With his hacking and child-custody court cases, Assange came up against both corporate and government systems he believed were not acting in the public's best interests. In college, he found himself involved with yet another institution not living up to its mandate. Then, through the two organizations he cocreated, Suburbia Public Access Network

A Good Father

In a December 2010 interview, Christine Hawkins, Assange's mother, said her son put his life and college education on hold to care for his newborn son. "He's a very good father," she said. "Not many men of that age will fight for their kids, but he stepped up to the responsibility."[9]

and Parent Inquiry Into Child Protection, Assange helped people expose classified information about authoritarian institutions. These experiences were leading Assange toward a Web site where whistle-blowers could safely reveal their secrets about authoritative regimes—WikiLeaks.

Assange did not enjoy his classes at the University of Melbourne.

Assange was concerned about the secrets governments kept from their citizens.

WikiLeaks

*I*n 2006, Assange began writing down his thoughts on individual rights versus authoritarian rule. On his blog, *IQ.org*, he published two essays addressing his philosophy. In "State and Terrorist Conspiracies," he wrote,

Where details are known as to the inner workings of authoritarian regimes, we see conspiratorial interactions among the political elite not merely for preferment or favor within the regime but as the primary planning methodology behind maintaining or strengthening authoritarian power. Authoritarian regimes give rise to forces which oppose them by pushing against the individual and collective will to freedom, truth and self realization.[1]

Assange went on to write that leaking secrets leaves institutions vulnerable to more open forms of government. In other words, if secrecy is a big part of illegitimate rule, then leaking those secrets could help keep rulers honest. These thoughts were the underlying philosophy of WikiLeaks.

STARTING WIKILEAKS

Obsessed with the idea for WikiLeaks, Assange shut himself in a house near the University of Melbourne. He worked long hours, often without sleeping or eating, to create the Web site. He let travelers live in the house for free in exchange for helping him build the site. His notes and flowcharts sometimes ended up on the walls and doors.

Constructing the Web site took Assange months. "The thing about Julian is that he is absolutely obsessively driven when he has a goal he wants to achieve," said his friend and author Suelette Dreyfus in an April 2010 interview. "So he basically dropped everything . . . enlisted a range of people from around the world and got them involved."[2]

Assange formed an advisory board of political, environmental, and human-rights activists, journalists, and computer specialists. He created Sunshine Press, a network of

What Is a Wiki?

A wiki is a collaborative Web site, which means users can freely edit, add to, and delete information. Probably the best-known wiki is Wikipedia, the online encyclopedia. The first wiki was created in 1995, and the word comes from the phrase *wiki wiki,* which means "quick" in Hawaiian. Wikis are popular with businesses whose employees are able to collaborate on projects, edit documents, and quickly exchange ideas. Educators use wikis for research projects and in the classroom for group learning.

While the openness of a wiki can result in users vandalizing the site by changing or deleting correct information and entering false data, wiki proponents say that same openness means wrong information can be quickly fixed. Skeptics note that it can take a long time for mistakes to get noticed and corrected, leaving users left wondering if what they are reading is really true. This is why wiki sites are often not accepted as legitimate research sources.

While most wikis are open to any user, limits can be set on access and editing. WikiLeaks, for example, is no longer a completely open wiki. While anyone can send documents to WikiLeaks, they do not instantly appear on the site until they have been analyzed.

people to support WikiLeaks. Rather than operate like a regular news organization, with reporters analyzing information and then writing stories about it, WikiLeaks would make raw data available and let others decide its meaning.

THE FIRST LEAKS

WikiLeaks posted its first document in December 2006. It was a message written by Somali rebel leader Sheikh Hassan Dahir Aweys, calling for the execution of government officials by criminals. The document was one of millions Assange came across as data was being retrieved by Chinese hackers over an encrypted server system.

While Assange was not sure if the Somali message was real, he posted it anyway. He hoped WikiLeaks readers would study it by using the site's interactive wiki capabilities. That never happened, but WikiLeaks got some news coverage due to the release. Assange was invited to talk about his Web site at the World Social Forum in Kenya on January 20, 2007. Assange would stay in Africa for two years.

Back to a Vagrant Lifestyle

Assange reverted to a vagrant lifestyle while living in Kenya. One of his friends said in an interview, "It would always be, 'Where is Julian?' It was always difficult to know where he was. It was almost like he was trying to hide."[3]

The first document posted on WikiLeaks was a message written by Sheikh Hassan Dahir Aweys, a Somali rebel leader.

In August 2007, the British newspaper the *Guardian* published a report—based on documents it obtained from WikiLeaks—on the Kenyan leader Daniel Arap Moi. The paper noted evidence that Moi and his allies embezzled billions of dollars

from the Kenyan government.
This supported the views that many
Kenyans already held about Moi.
The scandal helped sway the Kenyan
presidential election against Moi.
It would be the first WikiLeaks
document release to help spur
change.

The events in Kenya also gave
Assange his first taste of retaliation
against WikiLeaks. While sleeping
inside a guarded compound in the
country's capital of Nairobi one
night, six armed men sneaked in and
told Assange to lie on the ground.
Assange jumped up and shouted,
alerting the compound's security
team. The intruders fled. He was sure
they were after him.

MORE LEAKS, LEGAL THREATS, AND AWARDS

By 2008, just over one year
after being launched, the WikiLeaks
database had grown to 1.2 million

Death and Displacement in Kenya

Assange spoke in an interview about the violence that resulted from the 2007 uprising in Kenya in response to Moi's taking money from the government. Assange explained, "1,300 people were eventually killed, and 350,000 were displaced. That was a result of our leak. On the other hand, the Kenyan people had a right to that information and 40,000 children a year die of malaria in Kenya. And many more die of money being pulled out of Kenya, and as a result of the Kenyan shilling being debased."[4]

documents. Thousands of documents flooded in every day. However, the site was also drawing the wrath of leaders of the institutions whose documents were being exposed. This resulted in lawsuits and attempts to shut down the site.

In January 2008, WikiLeaks published secret documents of the Swiss bank Julius Baer. The documents alleged Julius Baer was helping clients avoid taxes and hide illegally gained money. The bank filed a suit against Dyandot, a California-based company that was WikiLeaks's domain name registrar. Julius Baer hoped to get at WikiLeaks through Dyandot. Through a US federal court, the bank asked that WikiLeaks be closed. The judge agreed, but soon reversed himself based on the First Amendment, which protects freedom of speech, and the fact that Julius Baer's documents could be easily accessed

"WikiLeaks is a non-profit media organization dedicated to bringing important news and information to the public. We provide an innovative, secure and anonymous way for independent sources around the world to leak information to our journalists. We publish material of ethical, political and historical significance while keeping the identity of our sources anonymous, thus providing a universal way for the revealing of suppressed and censored injustices."[5]
—*WikiLeaks's home page heading*

at any of WikiLeaks's many mirror sites. Jeffrey S. White, the judge in the case, said at the time of the trial, "We live in an age when people can do some good things and people can do some terrible things without accountability necessarily in a court of law."[6]

In February 2008, WikiLeaks drew the concern of the US military, and the attention of world governments, when it published the Pentagon's 2005 rules of engagement for troops in Iraq. This was a secret military document. It explained that US troops were allowed to pursue enemies into Iran and Syria. The US military called the leak of the classified document irresponsible. The US military said it put personnel at risk. WikiLeaks attracted more military anger when it published a classified operating manual for guided bombs that included information on the system's weaknesses.

In March 2008, WikiLeaks published a 612-page manual known as the bible of Scientology. It includes the writings of Scientology's founder, L. Ron Hubbard, on the basic principles of the religion. A month later, WikiLeaks posted a copyrighted and secret version of the Handbook of Instruction of the Church of Jesus Christ of Latter Day Saints—Mormons. Although WikiLeaks was threatened with lawsuits for

both leaks, Assange did not remove
the documents.

Lawsuits against WikiLeaks are
often dropped, or not attempted,
due to free-speech laws and the
negative publicity a lawsuit can
bring. By locating its original
computer servers in Sweden and
Belgium, two countries with strong
confidentiality laws, WikiLeaks took
advantage of the protection those
countries give to whistle-blowers.
The data flowing through WikiLeaks
is bounced around the Internet with
state-of-the-art encryption to hide
trails. If the main site is taken down,
there are so many duplicates, called
mirror sites, that WikiLeaks would
still be accessible. It has been said
that if someone wanted to get rid of
WikiLeaks entirely, they would have
to take down the Internet itself.

Although Assange was getting
lots of negative attention for the
secrets he was exposing, WikiLeaks's

"We're not that type of [political] activists. We are free-press activists. It's not about saving the whales. It's about giving the people the information they need to support whaling or not support whaling."[7]

—Assange,
60 Minutes *interview*,
aired January 30, 2011

campaign for transparency and free speech was also getting favorable notice. In 2008, Assange was awarded the Freedom of Expression Award from *Index on Censorship* magazine. Later, Amnesty International recognized Assange for his work in Kenya with its 2009 International UK Media Award.

THE WIKILEAKS ORGANIZATION

When WikiLeaks went public in December 2006, Assange claimed only that he was a member of the site's advisory board. A statement on the Web site explained that the site was "founded by Chinese dissidents, journalists, mathematicians and start-up company technologists from the US, Taiwan, Europe, Australia and South Africa."[8] In interviews, Assange said he was WikiLeaks's editor in chief. He claimed his goal as spokesperson was to deflect criticism away from the organization.

WikiLeaks's headquarters is set up in Sweden. WikiLeaks has a core group of about five full-time volunteer employees. It also has hundreds of other volunteers made up of journalists, computer programmers, and network engineers. Computer specialists maintain the computer servers and monitor the security and accessibility of the Web site. Journalists research leaked documents the site receives, making sure they are accurate.

Reliable material is material for which Assange or an associate has investigated the accuracy. This material is posted without editing and with a few comments. Assange has said he makes the final decision about releasing a document. The site's computerized drop box, which is not always operational, is highly encrypted to protect the person who downloads documents.

WikiLeaks is a nonprofit organization. It receives financing from donations. By the winter of 2009, donations had trickled to almost nothing. Assange toyed with a few ideas for getting money, including selling leaked documents. But he gave up those plans and put WikiLeaks into semi-dormancy. Assange's Web site was in danger of collapsing.

Assange claims he is the editor in chief at WikiLeaks.

*As the popularity of WikiLeaks grew,
the media wanted to find out more about Assange.*

AFGHAN WAR LOGS

y the end of 2009, the future of
WikiLeaks looked bleak. But after
the release of the *Collateral Murder* video on April 5,
2010 and heavy marketing, donations to WikiLeaks
skyrocketed. The site was fully operational again.

Along with the publicity over the video, attention swirled around Assange. Assange tried to keep the focus away from his personal life. This caused the media to wonder why a man dedicated to transparency was so quiet about himself. "What we want is transparent government, not transparent people," Assange told an interviewer. "One of our primary goals is to keep certain things secret, to keep the identities of sources secret."[1]

Staying Safe

The list of groups and governments rattled by WikiLeaks's revelations had grown since its public launch in December 2006. After the release of *Collateral Murder*, the criticism took on a more ominous tone against Assange and WikiLeaks. To avoid retaliation, Assange was constantly on the move. When he traveled back to Melbourne, Australia, in early May 2010, Australian police confiscated his passport at the airport. WikiLeaks had recently disclosed a confidential list of Web sites, including WikiLeaks, that the Australian government planned to ban. Assange's passport was quickly returned, but he added Australia to the list of countries where he could be arrested. The list also included Dubai,

Switzerland, and the Cayman Islands. He would soon add the United States to that list.

Bradley Manning

Since its public launch in 2006, WikiLeaks boasted that it had never revealed a source through its own actions. WikiLeaks did not, however, have any control over sources outing themselves. On May 26, 2010, the US Army's Criminal Investigation Division arrested US Army Private Bradley Manning, 22, at Contingency Operating Station Hammer, 40 miles (64.37 km) east of Baghdad, Iraq. Adrian Lamo, a former computer hacker whom Manning had chatted with online, had turned him in. Lamo said Manning took credit for leaking a number of items to WikiLeaks. The leaked items included the Iraq air-strike video, an Afghanistan air-strike video, an internal army report outlining WikiLeaks as a threat, and a cache of 260,000 classified US diplomatic cables.

In a transcript from one of his online chats to Lamo, Manning wrote, "If you had unprecedented access to classified networks 14 hours a day 7 days a week for 8+ months, what would you do?"[2] Manning wrote that the networks contained "incredible

Private Bradley Manning

things, awful things . . . that belonged in the public
domain, and not on some server stored in a dark
room in Washington DC."[3]

Now, billions of people had access to the same confidential information as Manning. Manning was not at liberty to share the information. An army spokesperson in an interview about Manning's situation explained,

> *If you have a security clearance and wittingly or unwittingly provide classified info to anyone who doesn't have security clearance or a need to know, you have violated security regulations and potentially the law.*[4]

After his arrest, Manning was taken to Kuwait. There, on July 6, 2010, he was charged with eight violations of federal criminal law and four noncriminal violations of US Army regulations. In April 2011, Manning was moved from the Quantico military jail in Virginia to a prison at Fort Leavenworth, Kansas. If convicted, he could be sentenced to life in prison.

A Foreshadowing of Manning's Arrest?

In March 2010, two months before Manning's arrest, WikiLeaks published an internal US Army counterintelligence report on the dangers that WikiLeaks posed to US soldiers. The report concluded that prosecuting WikiLeaks whistle-blowers would disrupt the site and discourage other potential whistle-blowers from sharing classified information.

Manhunt for Assange

After Manning's arrest, the Pentagon was aware that WikiLeaks had scores of documents in its possession that could damage national security. There was nothing the Pentagon could do to prevent the documents' release on WikiLeaks. However, the military wanted Assange's cooperation and to question him. If he was in the United States, the United States would have more legal options than if he was in a foreign country.

But Assange was not in the United

Whistle-blowers

WikiLeaks would not exist without whistle-blowers—individuals who release confidential information that suggests their employer or government is involved in some kind of fraud, corruption, or in some other way a threat to the public. Various US laws protect most whistle-blowers from retaliation, but not in all situations. While some people consider whistle-blowers tattletales and snitches, others see them as heroes.

One of the most famous US whistle-blowers is Daniel Ellsberg, a former military analyst. In 1969, having become convinced the US government was lying to the public about the war in Vietnam, he photocopied 7,000 pages of classified documents that were then published in the *New York Times* and other newspapers. The Pentagon papers leak embarrassed the government, added fuel to the antiwar movement, and helped contribute to the war's end.

In an interview about WikiLeaks, Ellsberg said,

I don't know who the source was, and if Bradley Manning is shown by the Army, beyond a reasonable doubt to be the source, he has my admiration and thanks for doing that. I faced that kind of risk myself forty years ago and it always seemed worthwhile to me to be willing to risk one's life in prison even to help shorten a war.[5]

States. He had gone into hiding after learning of Manning's arrest. Although Assange said in interviews he did not fear for his safety, he was constantly on alert. He would not travel to the United States or other countries where he might be arrested. Assange canceled a June 11 appearance at a Las Vegas, Nevada, conference and a July 17 appearance in New York City. Through his Twitter account, Assange wrote, "[It] looks like we're about to be attacked by everything the U.S. has."[6] While not admitting that Manning was the source of any leaked documents, Assange said WikiLeaks would hire lawyers to help defend him. In August 2010, WikiLeaks supporters announced they planned to hire an attorney for Manning.

"People have said I am anti-war: for the record, I am not. Sometimes nations need to go to war, and there are just wars. But there is nothing more wrong than a government lying to its people about those wars, then asking these same citizens to put their lives and their taxes on the line for those lies. If a war is justified, then tell the truth and the people will decide whether to support it."[7]

—*Assange, opinion piece in the* Australian, *December 7, 2010*

"Afghan War Diary"

By mid-July 2010, the statements coming from the US

State Department about Assange and WikiLeaks had become less negative. Assange made more public appearances. He was still concerned about security, though. He would not stay in the same place more than two nights in a row. While in hiding, he and his volunteers were preparing a collection of more than 90,000 records on the US war in Afghanistan. They released these records on July 25, 2010.

Titled the "Afghan War Diary," and generally referred to as the Afghan war logs, the documents were first made available to the *New York Times*, the *Guardian* newspaper in Great Britain, and *Der Spiegel* weekly in Germany. That way, reporters could analyze the material and publish articles simultaneously. It would be called the biggest leak in US military history. The Afghan war logs included many details:

- ❖ Coalition forces had killed hundreds of civilians in unreported incidents.

- ❖ Taliban attacks had soared.

- ❖ NATO commanders feared that Pakistan and Iran were fueling the insurgency.

- ❖ A special-forces unit hunted Taliban leaders and killed or captured them without trial.

❖ The United States covered up evidence the Taliban had acquired surface-to-air missiles.

❖ Unmanned drones were being increasingly used to hunt and kill Taliban by remote control.

❖ An escalation of Taliban roadside bombings had killed more than 2,000 civilians.

These leaks exposed some government conspiracies. They also may have put national security at risk. The White House quickly criticized WikiLeaks with a formal statement:

> We strongly condemn the disclosure of classified information by individuals and organizations, which puts the lives of the US and partner service members at risk and threatens our national security. WikiLeaks made no effort to contact the US government about these documents, which may contain information that endanger the lives of Americans, our partners, and local populations who co-operate with us.[8]

But Assange believed WikiLeaks had done its best to protect people involved in the Afghan war logs. The posted documents covered the period of the war between January 2004 and December 2009. Most were no longer militarily sensitive. Assange said in interviews that WikiLeaks withheld approximately

15,000 documents until he and his volunteers could delete the names of people whose safety might be in question. David Leigh, a reporter for the *Guardian*, spoke in an interview about the documents the three newspapers chose to publish:

> *We weren't going to publish anything which endangered individuals or genuinely compromised security. We knew most of the material was historic anyway. It was about operations that had already happened, so there wasn't any tactical sensitivity to it.*[9]

Speaking at a press conference at the Frontline Club in London, England, on July 26, Assange said the documents contained evidence of possible war crimes that should be investigated:

> *It is up to a court to decide, clearly, whether something is, in the end, a crime. That said. . . . there does appear to be evidence of war crimes in this material.*

"WikiLeaks has a four-year publishing history. During that time we have changed whole governments, but not a single person, as far as anyone is aware, has been harmed. . . . US Secretary of Defense Robert Gates admitted in a letter to the US congress that no sensitive intelligence sources or methods had been compromised by the Afghan war logs disclosure. The Pentagon stated there was no evidence the WikiLeaks reports had led to anyone being harmed in Afghanistan. NATO in Kabul told CNN it couldn't find a single person who needed protecting."[10]
—*Assange,*
on allegations that
WikiLeaks is harmful

"Seven days after the biggest intelligence leak of all time—the publication of over 75,000 files amounting to an entire history of the Afghanistan war—he is everywhere; in every newspaper, on every news broadcast, in what appears to be every country in the world. It's been an extraordinary week for WikiLeaks, which has seen the entrance on to the world stage of a remarkable new character: Assange."[12]

—*Carole Cadwalladr, reporter for the* Guardian

. . . It's important to understand, this material doesn't just reveal abuses. This material describes the past six years of war, every major attack that resulted in someone being detained or someone being killed.[11]

The reaction to the release of the Afghan war logs would continue for weeks. An avalanche of criticism and support would come from governments, media, and individuals around the world. The spotlight had turned again onto the human face of WikiLeaks. Not only was Assange out of hiding, he had catapulted to celebrity status.

Assange holds up the Guardian's report on the Afghan war logs.

Chairman of the Joint Chiefs of Staff Mike Mullen discussed the harmful effects of the Afghan war logs during a press conference on July 29, 2010.

IRAQ WAR LOGS

*A*s publicity churned around Assange in the days after the release of the Afghan war logs, supporters continued to see a human-rights crusader dedicated to exposing hidden truths, regardless of the consequences. Detractors saw a man driven by ego, thumbing his nose at the establishment, and uncaring of anyone who got harmed in the process.

WikiLeaks was called a criminal project. US officials found some names in the Afghan war logs that should have been removed. They believed the damage done to national security could not be reversed. Some said the Web site should be shut down. It was suggested that Manning, if convicted of leaking documents to WikiLeaks, should face the death penalty for treason.

The United States promised a thorough FBI investigation into the source of the leaks, suspecting Manning had people helping him. Officials were also exploring ways to prosecute Assange. If Assange had solicited Manning for the material, there would be a clearer case for espionage. The Obama administration asked Britain, Germany, Australia, and other Western governments to look into opening criminal investigations against Assange and to limit his travel across their borders.

Because of the possibility that innocent people might be harmed by the leaks, some organizations that had been supportive of WikiLeaks, including Amnesty International, withdrew their support. They condemned Assange for not being more careful in editing the classified material. Mike Mullen, chairman of the Joint Chiefs of Staff, a military advisory group to the president, said on July 29, 2010, that the leakers "might already have on their hands the blood of some young soldier or that of an Afghan family."[1] To that accusation, Assange replied in a television interview, saying,

> It's really quite fantastic that [US Secretary of Defense] Gates and Mullen . . . who have ordered assassinations every day, are trying to bring people on board to look at a speculative understanding of whether we might have blood on our hands.[2]

RAPE ALLEGATIONS

On August 11, 2010, Assange traveled to Stockholm, Sweden, where he attended a conference. He also applied for Swedish residency and a work visa. Because of Sweden's history of strong support for press freedoms, it would be an ideal place for Assange to create a secure base for WikiLeaks. But on August 21, a story leaked to the press that Assange was sought in Sweden on allegations of rape. About learning of the accusations, Assange said in an interview, "It was shocking. I have been accused of various things in recent years, but nothing so serious as this."[3]

Then, within a day, Stockholm police reversed themselves, saying the allegations were dropped. According to one of the two women involved in the accusations, neither she nor the other woman who went to the police had intended for Assange to be charged with rape. But, she said in an interview that Assange had, "attitude problems with women."[4]

She also denied claims by Assange and his supporters that the allegations were part of a smear campaign to discredit him. Assange said he had been warned the Pentagon or CIA might use dirty tricks on him, including a sex trap. On September 1, a Swedish prosecutor reopened the rape investigation.

The negative attention caused members of the WikiLeaks organization, including Birgitta Jonsdottir, a member of the Icelandic parliament, to wonder if Assange

The WikiLeaks War Room

US officials revealed in August 2010 that approximately 120 FBI agents, intelligence analysts, and others were working around the clock in a suburban Virginia office they called the WikiLeaks War Room. Formally known as the Information Review Task Force, it was headed by Brigadier General Robert A. Carr of the Defense Intelligence Agency. The office's task was to figure out what information might have been leaked to WikiLeaks, what risks the information posed, and to gather evidence that could be used to prosecute Assange on possible future espionage charges, including evidence of contact between WikiLeaks and alleged leaker Manning.

should step aside as WikiLeaks's spokesperson. "Julian is brilliant in many ways," Jonsdottir told an interviewer, "but he doesn't have very good social skills. And . . . he's a bit of a male chauvinist."[5] An anonymous WikiLeaks member said that Assange's insistence on staying in charge was creating a lot of problems just as they were getting ready to release more documents. WikiLeaks technicians temporarily shut down the Web site as a message to Assange to reconsider what he was doing.

"No one has been harmed, but should anyone come to harm of course that would be a matter of deep regret—our goal is justice to innocents, not to harm them. That said, if we were forced into a position of publishing all of the archives or none of the archives we would publish all . . . because it's extremely important to the history of this war."[6]

—*Assange, regarding accusations of possible harm as a result of the Afghan war logs release*

By mid-September 2010, Assange was told by Swedish police that he was free to leave Sweden while an investigation was still under way. There was no warrant for his arrest, nor was he wanted for questioning. He was also informed that his Swedish residency and work permit applications had been denied. Assange left for London.

INTERNAL REVOLT

Key WikiLeaks volunteers were upset about more than the rape allegations against Assange.

When Assange announced that WikiLeaks would be releasing 392,000 classified documents on the Iraq war in October 2010, some WikiLeaks staffers believed this was too soon. They feared it did not leave enough time to remove the names of US collaborators and informants in Iraq who might be in danger of retaliation. There were also complaints about Assange publishing big, splashy leaks rather than smaller leaks, which was the Web site's original purpose. The WikiLeaks

The US Legal Case against Assange

While some Americans have accused Assange of treason, the accusation is not really accurate since the definition of treason is a crime against one's own country. Assange could only be tried for treason in his home country of Australia, and then he would need to return there to be arrested.

There is one US law that Assange might have broken, which US government agencies were investigating—the Espionage Act of 1917. This law allows for prison sentences and even the death penalty for publishing information that interferes with US military operations. The Espionage Act was passed during World War I, has seldom been used, and it is unclear how today's courts would interpret the law. Some experts have said the Espionage Act and other US espionage laws are outdated and not meant to deal with mass Internet leaks.

The United States could try to change the law to make prosecuting Assange easier, and some politicians and military leaders have suggested doing just that. But the US Constitution provides so many protections under the First Amendment to publishers of state secrets—as opposed to sources, who can be prosecuted—that it would be difficult to do. Plus, any law that applied to Assange and WikiLeaks would also apply to other publishers of WikiLeaks documents, including the *New York Times*.

encrypted submission portal was taken offline for a
month while staff readied the next big release. This
upset some volunteers.

Staff member Daniel Domscheit-Berg, also known
as Daniel Schmitt, served as the German spokesperson
for WikiLeaks. In a e-mail, Domscheit-Berg had
accused Assange of behaving like an emperor. In
response, Assange suspended Domscheit-Berg for a
month. Domscheit-Berg eventually resigned from
WikiLeaks. An Icelandic WikiLeaks volunteer named
Herbert Snorrason questioned Assange about his
treatment of Domscheit-Berg. Assange replied
online to Snorrason:

> *I am the heart and soul of this organization, its founder,
> philosopher, spokesperson, original coder, organizer, financier
> and all the rest. If you have a problem with me, piss off.*[7]

Snorrason thought Assange was pushing the most
capable WikiLeaks volunteers away.

More War Logs

Despite the internal struggles, Assange and
WikiLeaks volunteers continued to work in London
on what was called the Iraq war logs. This included
almost 400,000 classified US military field reports

covering the war in Iraq from 2004 to 2009. Assange modified his process this time, removing every name from the documents before their release. Assange said he sent a request to the Pentagon asking for suggestions on how to further minimize harm. However, the Pentagon claimed the request was never received.

As he had with the Afghan war logs, Assange released the huge cache of documents to selected news agencies weeks earlier. This gave the news agencies time to analyze the material. Then, on October 22, 2010, the documents were posted on WikiLeaks and published in participating newspapers. It became the largest intelligence leak in US history. Among its many details, the Iraq war logs revealed critical information about the behavior of military personnel and the loss of civilian life:

An Air of Tension

Reporter Isabelle Fraser wrote about her October 2010 weekend as a WikiLeaks volunteer right before the Iraq war logs were released. She was told by WikiLeaks's staff not to tell anyone about her weekend or where she was going. Afterward, Fraser wrote a report about volunteering at WikiLeaks. Fraser described an us-versus-them atmosphere. "There is an air of tension among the WikiLeaks people that I meet. Many wonder whether they are being bugged or followed."[8] Fraser noted that one activist in the small London office hid herself under a blanket as she typed a password into her computer.

❖ Hundreds of reports of abuse, torture, rape, and murder by Iraqi police and soldiers were never investigated.

❖ The US helicopter involved in the air strike featured in the *Collateral Murder* video had previously killed Iraqi insurgents after they tried to surrender.

❖ Fifteen thousand more civilians died than the US government had reported.

While WikiLeaks staff had removed all sensitive names from the documents, and the Pentagon admitted the Afghan war logs had not resulted in any known casualties, the Pentagon condemned the new leaks for similar reasons. US troops and their allies could get killed. Enemies could use the classified information in their fight against the United States. Assange was squarely in the middle of a swarming controversy again. And, the controversy would become even more complicated in the coming weeks. ⌐

Julian Assange

Assange discusses the Iraq war logs
at a press conference on October 23, 2010.

INTERPOL

DIPC ICPO

INTERPOL

7 December 2010

Home

About INTERPOL

News

Drugs

Criminal organizations

Pharmaceutical crime

Financial and high-tech crime

Intellectual Property

Wanted

ASSANGE, Julian Paul

2010852105 ASSANGE JULIAN PAUL

*Interpol issued a red notice for Assange in November 2010.
That meant that if he was caught he would face arrest in Britain.*

CABLEGATE

O n October 23, 2010, Assange was
answering questions on a British
CNN news program. The host asked him about
the internal problems at WikiLeaks and about the
Swedish sex-abuse allegations. Disgusted, Assange

removed his microphone and walked off the set. He accused the interviewer of not wanting to talk about the Iraq war logs, which had just been released on WikiLeaks.

This would not be the only interview to slide from the subject of the leaks to Assange. Assange expected outrage over the newest leaks, but the outrage centered on him. There were more calls for his arrest and more suggestions that he be stopped by any means possible, including with his assassination.

Meanwhile, the Swedish investigation into Assange's alleged sexual misconduct continued. In early November 2010, Assange told a Swedish newspaper he was suing for damages the accusations had caused to his reputation. Fearing again for his safety, Assange, who was living in London, considered seeking asylum in Switzerland.

In a bit of good news, Assange was nominated in November for *Time* magazine's 2010 Person of the Year. But any celebrating would have been short-lived. On November 18, Swedish police announced that an international arrest warrant would be issued for Assange. A judge had finally indicted him for rape, sexual molestation, and unlawful coercion. The Swedish prosecutor wanted to extradite Assange

**Whistle-blower
for the Digital Age**

In nominating Assange as its 2010 Person of the Year in November, *Time* magazine said, "He is a new kind of whistle-blower: one made for the digital age."[2] Although Assange would be the clear winner in the readers' choice poll, the magazine chose Mark Zuckerberg, cofounder and chief executive officer of the social networking site Facebook.

to Sweden for questioning. Assange's attorney appealed the extradition, but the appeal was rejected. The arrest warrant triggered a red notice from Interpol, an international policing organization. A red notice alerts authorities to monitor a person's travels. This meant that Assange would face arrest in Britain if Interpol caught him.

Whatever personal issues Assange faced, they did not keep him from his quest for transparency. Toward the end of November 2010, he announced a few upcoming WikiLeaks releases. He said these releases would include confidential documents from Russia, China, and—the major release—a fresh batch of previously classified US government documents. "Next release is 7x the [word count] size of the Iraq War Logs," someone from WikiLeaks said via a Twitter message on November 22. "Intense pressure over it for months. Hold us powerful."[1]

CABLEGATE

The group of documents contained 251,287 confidential messages passed between the US State Department and more than 270 foreign field offices around the world. Aware for weeks of the content of the possible leak, the United States warned Assange that publishing the cables might be illegal and would endanger countless lives and harm international cooperation. The State Department sent Assange a letter requesting that he not post the documents on WikiLeaks and that he return the material to the United States. Assange told the US ambassador to Britain that WikiLeaks would not bend to Washington's pressure.

Again, WikiLeaks provided the cables to five international news outlets, including the *New York Times*, a few weeks before they were posted to WikiLeaks. The *New York Times* took care to redact information that could be harmful to people or countries. It sent the Obama administration the cables it planned to release and made some changes based on the administration's feedback.

On November 28, 2010, the international news outlets published articles on a set of 1,900 confidential diplomatic cables from the

Many newspapers reported on the leaked diplomatic cables.

entire group. The document dump was nicknamed
Cablegate. Unlike previous big releases, the
documents were not posted simultaneously on

WikiLeaks. At the time, WikiLeaks was under
a denial-of-service cyber attack, being flooded
with requests for information that made the site
unavailable to users.

Officials in the Obama administration had
already warned US allies that the content of the
cables could be embarrassing. Some of the cables
contained blunt descriptions of other country's
leaders and allegations of corruption.
By the Monday following the release,
the public had learned a variety of
information about the United States
and its foreign affairs, including
details about the Middle East:

* The United States believed
  Iran obtained missiles from
  North Korea that are capable of
  striking Western Europe.

* Saudi Arabia wanted the United
  States to intervene against Iran
  but was unwilling to do so itself.

* The United States was struggling
  with Pakistan over its nuclear
  missiles.

Cablegate, Watergate

The name *Cablegate* is
a take-off on *Watergate*,
the name for a politi-
cal scandal of the 1970s
in which five men were
arrested for breaking into
the Democratic National
Committee headquarters
at the Watergate Complex
in Washington DC. The
arrests led to the resigna-
tion of President Richard
M. Nixon after it was
revealed, through his own
secret tape recordings,
that he had tried to cover
up his connection to the
break-in. Since then, the
suffix *-gate* has been used
to suggest a scandal, usu-
ally involving dishonest
behavior or a cover-up.

Response to Cablegate

At a news conference, Secretary of State Hillary Clinton said the United States deeply regretted the alleged leaks. She said they were "an attack on both the United States and the entire international community."[3] She also explained that the cables did not represent US foreign policy. Some foreign governments expressed anger over the leaks. Others tried to play down their release. The full effects would take time to unfold. As the author of one article noted, "Would Italian voters tolerate a Prime Minister who, by the U.S. ambassador's account, appeared to be 'profiting personally and handsomely' from sweetheart energy deals with Russia?"[4]

Although none of the cables posted on WikiLeaks were top secret, Clinton brought up an argument that would be echoed in the coming weeks: In the course of doing their jobs in promoting US national security, US diplomats counted on the candid insights of people inside and outside of foreign governments. If those sources thought the information they shared could not be kept confidential, they would not be so open in the future.

Many citizens in the United States and abroad also expressed their disapproval of the release of secret documents. Some people complained the documents did not really provide any new information. Despite name and date changes the news outlets made to the documents, some readers

Diplomatic Oddities

In addition to more serious revelations, the diplomatic cables released on WikiLeaks revealed a few odd events and personality quirks of international leaders. The *Christian Science Monitor* newspaper listed their top five strange stories from Cablegate:

1. Chechen President Ramzan Kadyrov danced at a wedding with a gold-plated gun stuck down the back of his jeans.
2. King Abdullah of Saudi Arabia suggested that the US government track detainees released from the Guantanamo Bay prison with the same surgically implanted tracking chips used in horses and falcons.
3. President Ali Adfullah Saleh, the ruler of Yemen, which bans alcohol consumption, said he did not care if whiskey was smuggled into his country as long as it was good whiskey.
4. A US citizen of Iranian descent was visiting family in Iran. When he tried to return to the United States, his passport was confiscated and he was ordered to pay a fine and instruct his music-promoter sons in Los Angeles to cancel a concert in Dubai by a popular Persian pop group.
5. Libyan leader Mu'ammar Gadhafi stays only on the first floor, likes to conduct meetings outside in a Bedouin tent, dislikes flying over water, is a fan of flamenco dancing, and is accompanied everywhere he goes by a blond nurse.

worried the cables still put lives at risk. Others felt the news outlets compromised their credibility by working with WikiLeaks.

Still, in hiding and fearing for his safety, Assange participated in interviews about the cables' release by e-mail and phone. He wrote to ABC News via e-mail on November 29, dismissing claims that people's lives were in danger, "U.S. officials have for 50 years trotted out this line when they are afraid the public is going to see how they really behave."[6] Alluding to the fact that WikiLeaks still held many more cables yet to publish, he wrote, "We're only one thousandth of the way in and look at what has so far [been] revealed. There will be many more."[7]

Beautiful and Horrifying

Revealing in an online chat that he had allegedly leaked classified documents, Manning wrote, "Hillary Clinton and several thousand diplomats around the world are going to have a heart attack when they wake up one morning, and find an entire repository of classified foreign policy is available, in searchable format, to the public. . . . Everywhere there's a U.S. post, there's a diplomatic scandal that will be revealed. It's open diplomacy. . . . It's beautiful, and horrifying."[8]

On November 29, 2010, Secretary of State Hillary Clinton answered questions about WikiLeaks's recent release of confidential US documents.

In early December 2010, Assange worried that he would be extradited from England to stand trial in Sweden.

HIDING AND ARREST

s the Swedish warrant for Assange wound its way through the Interpol police system in early December 2010, the United States announced it was further investigating whether Assange had violated the Espionage Act by releasing the diplomatic cables. Assange was keeping a low profile in England. From there, he and his lawyers hoped to succeed with another appeal to the Swedish courts to avoid extradition to their country. Assange was convinced the extradition was motivated by pressure from the United States. He felt that if he ended up in Sweden, he would be sent to the United States.

Assange considered taking refuge in another country. In late November, the deputy foreign minister of Ecuador, Kintto Lucas, offered Assange refuge there. But Ecuador's president, Rafael Correa, took back the welcome. Returning to Australia was doubtful, since the Australian attorney general was exploring whether Assange had broken any of that country's laws, too. Wherever he went, Assange would have difficulty traveling. Showing his passport at any border might get him arrested.

Insurance Package

While fearing for his safety in July 2010, Assange posted a mysterious document on WikiLeaks titled "insurance.aes256." More than 100,000 people around the world downloaded the file, which is encrypted and cannot be read without a key. In December 2010, Assange explained in interviews the purpose of the file: if anything should happen to him or WikiLeaks, the encryption key would automatically be released. He said the file contained the entire archive of diplomatic cables and other confidential material from the United States and other countries.

Nine Days in Jail

Exhausted by the legal stresses and the task of running WikiLeaks after key volunteers had left, Assange walked into a London police station on December 7, 2010. There, he was arrested on the Swedish warrant. After spending nine days in jail, Assange was released on December 16 on $300,000 bail, paid at least in part by a group of celebrities, including US filmmaker and activist Michael Moore. As he walked out of jail, Assange told reporters,

> *I hope to continue my work and continue to protest my innocence in this matter and to reveal, as we get it, which we have not yet, the evidence from these allegations.[1]*

Assange moved into a ten-bedroom mansion in eastern England owned by a supporter named Vaughan Smith, owner of London's Frontline Club. The conditions of Assange's bail would mostly keep him from leaving Smith's home. This ended, at least temporarily, his nomadic lifestyle.

"When it comes to the point where you occasionally look forward to being in prison on the basis that you might be able to spend a day reading a book, the realization dawns that perhaps the situation has become a little more stressful than you would like."[2]

—*Assange, quoted in a* New York Times *article, October 23, 2010*

*Reporters swarming around a van carrying Assange
from court during his nine days in jail*

Personal, Cyber, and Corporate Reprisals

After release of the diplomatic cables, the clamor
against Assange became more heated. Threats against
his life came from within and without governments.
Tom Flanagan, a former adviser to the prime
minister of Canada, called for Assange to be killed.
In the United States, Republican politician Mike
Huckabee said, "Anything less than execution [for
Assange] is too kind a penalty."[3]

There were demands to shut down the WikiLeaks
site, including from US Senator Joe Lieberman,

Unexpected Support

While Assange had supporters in the United States, not many of them were politicians willing to speak up on his behalf. But in December 2010, Republican Ron Paul, representative from Texas, argued that Assange should get the same protection as other media. "In a free society we're supposed to know the truth. In a society where truth becomes treason, then we're in big trouble," he said on a television news program.[4] Said Democrat John Conyers, representative from Michigan, "Unpopularity is not a crime and publishing offensive information isn't either."[5]

chairman of the Senate Homeland Security Committee. While shutting down WikiLeaks was not literally possible, Amazon, a major Web-hosting provider, dropped WikiLeaks from its servers after receiving a telephone call from Lieberman. Other companies with connections to WikiLeaks also ended their relationships. The Swiss financial firm PostFinance closed Assange's account, saying he had lied about his residency status. PayPal, the online payment system, refused to allow payments through WikiLeaks, saying the site promoted illegal activity. Credit card companies Visa and MasterCard also began blocking payments to WikiLeaks. Bank of America followed suit.

The attempts to keep WikiLeaks from functioning alarmed free-speech groups and activists. They claimed the actions amounted to censorship. In retaliation, members of the hacktivist group Anonymous bombarded PayPal, Amazon, and other companies that had dropped WikiLeaks with denial-of-service attacks. There were signs that WikiLeaks was again close to collapse. It still was not accepting new online submissions from potential whistle-blowers. And, it was short of cash, mainly because its donation processors had stopped providing service.

On January 10, 2011, Assange said he might move to Switzerland, though he had

Sounding Off against Assange

Politicians sounded off against Assange, WikiLeaks, and the Obama administration's handling of events. Sarah Palin said on her Facebook page in November 2010,

Assange is an anti-American operative with blood on his hands. His past posting of classified documents revealed the identity of more than 100 Afghan sources to the Taliban. Why was he not pursued with the same urgency we pursue al Qaeda and Taliban leaders?[6]

Palin directed readers to an editorial by William Kristol, former chief of staff to former vice president Dan Quayle:

Why can't we use our various assets to harass, snatch or neutralize Julian Assange and his collaborators, wherever they are? Why can't we disrupt and destroy Wiki-Leaks in both cyberspace and physical space, to the extent possible?[7]

Criticism also came from Democrats. Bob Beckel, a consultant for the Democratic Party, said on a television news program:

This guy's a traitor, treasonous, and he has broken every law of the United States. The guy ought to be—and I'm not for the death penalty—so if I'm not for the death penalty, there's only one way to do it: illegally shoot [him].[8]

**Anonymous and
Denial of Service Attacks**

Anonymous, the
organization that retaliated
against companies that
discontinued service to
WikiLeaks, is a loose-knit
group of approximately
1,000 Internet freedom
fighters who formed from
the anarchic message
board 4chan. According to
its Web site, while Anonymous is not affiliated with
WikiLeaks, the group
shares the same goals
of transparency and free
speech online. In addition
to mirroring the WikiLeaks
site and political lobbying
on its behalf, Anonymous
members have bombarded
companies such as PayPal
and Amazon with denial-
of-service attacks, where
hundreds of automated
load requests are made to
a Web site. This activity
overloads the site's server,
essentially shutting down
the site for business.

not made a request for political asylum. US officials were seeking information from the Twitter accounts of WikiLeaks volunteers. But Assange insisted he would keep posting documents. He set up shop in Smith's home, gathered a few volunteers around him, and continued working.

Assange speaks to reporters outside of Smith's home, Ellingham Hall.

Assange's former colleague, Daniel Domscheit-Berg, is now founder of OpenLeaks.

WikiLeaks Revolution

Although Assange was required to stay in London on bail, the WikiLeaks's releases continued to impact the world. Tunisia was one country that was affected. Tunisia is a small country in North Africa, situated between Algeria and

Libya. It has had many serious problems, including rising food prices, government corruption, and high unemployment. Tunisians have often voiced their frustrations by taking to the streets and protesting.

Within the Cablegate documents released on November 28, 2010, were diplomatic cables supporting protestors' suspicions that their government was corrupt. With this release, unrest grew in Tunisia. Tunisian authorities tried to block access to WikiLeaks. They started seeking out activists and dissidents via social networking sites for punishment. In response, riots broke out throughout the country. Reacting to the increasing violence, the Tunisian president, Zine El Abidine Ben Ali, fled the country in January 2011.

While Tunisia had problems long before WikiLeaks released the Cablegate documents, it could be said that the leaks triggered public action. They confirmed what Tunisians already suspected, but for which they had no proof. What happened in Tunisia set an example for other

Avoid Temptation, Avoid WikiLeaks

In advising corporations on how to handle document leaks, WikiLeaks staffer Kristinn Hrafnsson suggests simply, "[The corporation] should resist the temptation to enter into corruption."[1] And Don Tapscott, who cowrote the book *The Naked Corporation*, gives this advice to worried companies: "Open your own kimono. You're going to be naked. So you have to dig deep, look at your whole operation, make sure that integrity is part of your bones."[2]

African and Middle Eastern countries. Egypt, Algeria, Jordan, Sudan, and Yemen all experienced different levels of protests and uprisings related to seeking more democratic forms of government.

WikiLeaks Spin-offs and Copycats

Daniel Domscheit-Berg announced the start of his own leak-hosting site in January 2011. With OpenLeaks, Domscheit-Berg said he hoped to avoid some of the mistakes he believed Assange made, such as publishing raw information and then leaving it for others to sort through. Rather than publishing the leaks, Domscheit-Berg plans to link leakers with groups that can make use of the leaks. Included on the OpenLeaks's staff is another defector from WikiLeaks code-named the Architect, a programmer said to be as skilled as Assange.

Some other new leak-hosting sites specialize in certain regions or topics, including Russia, the European Union, international trade, and the

Iceland: The Friendliest Whistle-blower Country

In June 2010, Iceland's parliament unanimously passed a proposal to introduce new legislation that would bring strong source-protection, freedom of information, and transparency laws to the country. Known as the Icelandic Modern Media Initiative, once completed, the laws would make Iceland the most whistle-blower friendly country on Earth. Birgitta Jonsdottir, former WikiLeaks volunteer and an Icelandic parliament member, spearheaded the proposal, which Assange and WikiLeaks helped create.

pharmaceutical industry. The site GreenLeaks focuses on leaks regarding the environment, climate, and natural resources. Some news organizations, such as the *New York Times*, are exploring the creation of Web-based methods for receiving leaks directly, so they can cut out middlemen like Assange.

When asked about possible competitors to WikiLeaks, Assange told a reporter,

> The supply of leaks is very large. It's helpful for us to have more people in this industry. It's protective to us. It's not something that's easy to do right. . . . It's very easy and very dangerous to do it wrong.[3]

Cybersecurity

A 2009 study found that 60 percent of former corporate employees took sensitive data with them before they left their companies. To combat confidential information from finding its way from employees and hackers onto sites such as WikiLeaks, more and more corporations are turning to leak-focused security. Cybersecurity will likely continue to grow as an industry, helped in part by government-funded research and former hackers who have switched to the security business. For his part, Assange does not believe even the most sophisticated cybersecurity can stop a determined and highly motivated person from retrieving data.

CORPORATE LEAKS

In early October 2010, WikiLeaks shut down its document-submission system due to cyber attacks. WikiLeaks also did not have the manpower to process all of the documents it was receiving. But Assange still had a huge cache of secrets yet to expose, some of which related to corporations and the private sector, including banks.

At a press conference on January 17, 2011, Rudolf Elmer, a former employee of the Swiss bank Julius Baer, handed two CDs to Assange. The CDs contained 2,000 names and account details belonging to celebrities, business leaders, and politicians Elmer said were using offshore bank accounts to avoid paying taxes. At the press conference, Assange said he would post the data on WikiLeaks once he had the chance to analyze it.

Assange claimed that over the coming months he would be posting more corporate "megaleaks" on pharmaceutical companies, energy corporations (including an oil firm that he said sabotaged its competitor's wells), and more financial firms. These leaks could have a large effect on those who receive them. For example, when it was rumored that WikiLeaks was in possession of a five-gigabyte hard drive belonging to a

WikiLeaks Wish List

Asked by a reporter if he had a wish list of the type of leaked information he was looking for next, Assange said, "All governments, all industries. We accept all material of diplomatic, historical or ethical significance that hasn't been released before and is under active suppression. There's a question about which industries have the greatest potential for reform. Those may be the ones we haven't heard about yet. So what's the big thing around the corner? The real answer is I don't know. No one in the public knows. But someone on the inside does know."[4]

Supporters of Assange stand outside Belmarsh Magistrates' Court, while a judge ruled that Assange should be extradited to Sweden.

Bank of America executive, the bank's stock price fell 3 to 5 percent.

Leaks to Come

Because approximately 1,900 of the 250,000 diplomatic cables were released in November 2010, a huge number of confidential documents still remained to be released to the public. Assange, in an agreement with the five original news publications he had given the entire set of documents to in November, was planning to release further cables following a set time frame. In December 2010,

the Norwegian newspaper *Aftenposten* announced it
had obtained all 250,000 documents and planned
to release specific diplomatic cables that it would
publish on its own schedule with related in-depth
articles. It was unclear what the remaining Cablegate
documents contained, but the topics could be far-
reaching. In an online chat hosted by the *Guardian*
newspaper in December 2010, Assange said there
were references to UFOs contained within the
archive. He told another newspaper he had cables
relating to Rupert Murdoch and his company, News
Corporation.

THE FUTURE FOR ASSANGE

In December 2010, Assange announced he
would be authoring an autobiography to help fund
WikiLeaks and pay his mounting legal bills. Alfred
A. Knopf, a major book publisher, acknowledged
it would be publishing Assange's work. According
to Assange, he was not writing a book because he
wanted to, but because he needed the $1.5 million
he was being paid to do so. A multitude of films and
biographies about Assange were also in the works.

The possibility that the United Statues would try to
extradite Assange lessened when, in late January 2011,

US military sources said their investigation had revealed no evidence of a direct link between Assange and Manning. Without that link, the United States would have difficulty extraditing or prosecuting Assange. However, on February 25, 2011, a judge ruled that Assange should be extradited to Sweden to face the rape and sexual molestation allegations. Assange appealed the judge's ruling. A two-day hearing was set to begin on July 12, 2011, in London.

Despite his financial and legal problems, the

Assange's Family

As of December 2010, Assange's mother, Christine Hawkins, was living in Australia on the Sunshine Coast. Working as a puppeteer, she performed puppet plays at birthday parties and schools. She had never owned a computer, telling an interviewer, "I don't like technology generally." She said of her son, "Julian was brave. And for him to stand up for what he believes in makes me happy as a mother."[5]

Assange's son, Daniel, received a bachelor of science degree from the University of Melbourne. As of February 2011, he was working as a software engineer in Melbourne. When his father first started WikiLeaks, he asked Daniel if he wanted to join him in his Web site venture. Daniel declined, thinking his father would not succeed. Since then, Daniel has changed his mind, telling an interviewer that he has "much respect for my father and his cause."[6] According to Daniel, his father had not been in touch with him for a few years. Daniel had received death threats and assumed his father was keeping his distance partly to protect him.

Brett, Assange's stepfather, was retired and living in Sydney, Australia. He said of his stepson,

He always stood up for the underdog. I remember that, like with his school friends. He was always very angry about people ganging up on other people. I wholeheartedly support him in everything he's doing.[7]

Stirring Things Up

When an interviewer mentioned to Assange that he seemed to enjoy stirring things up, Assange smiled before replying, "When you see abusive organizations suffer the consequences as a result of their abuse, and you see victims elevated, yes, that's a very pleasurable activity to be involved in."[8]

end of 2010 and beginning of 2011 brought some positive recognition for Assange and WikiLeaks. Senior editors at Postmedia Network newspapers voted him top newsmaker of 2010 for his impact on information delivery. *Le Monde* newspaper in France named Assange its 2010 Man of the Year based on a public online vote. He was awarded the Gold Medal by the Sydney Peace Foundation, which it had given only to three other people in the foundation's 14-year history. And it was announced in February that Assange had been nominated for the 2011 Nobel Peace Prize.

The problems and acclaim were a fitting summary of Assange's life. Whether considered an arrogant zealot or a heroic freedom fighter, loved or hated, admired or demonized, most would agree that the impact of Julian Assange and his Web site, WikiLeaks, was an important one that would be felt for a long time. The vagabond boy from Australia with a love of computers had changed the shape of the information landscape.

Assange attended a debate about whistle-blowing in London on April 9, 2011.

TIMELINE

1971	1984	1987
Julian Assange is born on July 3 in Townsville, Australia.	Assange gets his first computer.	Assange begins hacking.

1996	1997	2003
Assange pleads guilty to the Nortel hacking charges on December 5.	Assange cowrites *Underground: Tales of Hacking, Madness, and Obsession on the Electronic Frontier.*	Assange begins attending the University of Melbourne, where he will take classes for three years.

1989	1991	1993
Assange marries but soon divorces.	Assange is arrested by police in Melbourne, Australia, for hacking into the Canadian telecom company Nortel.	Assange helps establish Suburbia Public Access Network.

2006	2007	2009
Assange creates WikiLeaks, which releases its first document in December.	In January, Assange speaks publicly about WikiLeaks at a conference in Kenya.	Assange receives the International UK Media Award from Amnesty International for his work in Kenya.

TIMELINE

2010

On April 5,
WikiLeaks releases
an Iraq air-strike
video titled
Collateral Murder.

2010

On May 26,
US Army Private
Bradley Manning is
arrested for allegedly
leaking secret
military documents
to WikiLeaks.

2010

On July 25,
WikiLeaks releases
approximately
91,000 US military
documents referred
to as the Afghan
war logs.

2010

On November 18,
Swedish courts issue
an international arrest
warrant for Assange
related to alleged
sexual assaults.

2010

On November 28,
1,900 confidential
US diplomatic cables
are released, which
will come to be
called Cablegate.

2010

In December, Assange
surrenders to British
police and is taken
into custody over
sex-abuse charges.
He is released on bail
on December 16.

2010

2010

2010

From August 21
to August 22,
Swedish police open,
then quickly close,
an investigation into
allegations of sexual
assault by Assange.

The Swedish sexual
assault case against
Assange is reopened
on September 1.

The Iraq war logs,
nearly 400,000
confidential US
military reports about
the war in Iraq, is
posted on WikiLeaks
on October 22.

2010

2011

2011

Assange is named
2010 Man of the Year
by *Le Monde*
newspaper in France.

Assange is nominated
for the 2011 Nobel
Peace Prize.

In May,
Assange is awarded
the Gold Medal
from the Sydney
Peace Foundation.

Essential Facts

Date of Birth

July 3, 1971

Place of Birth

Townsville, Queensland, Australia

Parents

Christine Hawkins and Brett Assange (stepfather); John Shipton (biological father)

Education

Assange attended many schools because his family moved so frequently. He was also homeschooled by his mother. From 2003 to 2006, Assange took some college courses at the University of Melbourne but never graduated.

Marriage

1989, divorced soon after

Children

Daniel

CAREER HIGHLIGHTS

Assange was awarded the Freedom of Expression Award from the *Index on Censorship* magazine in 2008. In 2009, he received the International UK Media Award from Amnesty International. The Sydney Peace Foundation awarded him with the Peace Medal in 2010. He was nominated for the 2011 Nobel Peace Prize.

SOCIETAL CONTRIBUTION

In 2006, Assange combined his computer expertise and a growing interest in promoting institutional transparency in the creation of WikiLeaks, a Web site designed to give whistle-blowers a safe place to reveal secrets. Advocates of WikiLeaks believe Assange is an important crusader for government transparency around the world.

CONFLICTS

Conflict for Assange began early in his life, when, at the age of eight, he, his mother, and half brother fled from his stepfather and went into hiding. Assange was arrested in 1991 for his hacking activity, and his marriage ended, leading to depression and a long custody battle for his son. Since cofounding WikiLeaks in 2006, Assange has been in conflict with governments, corporations, institutions, and individuals angry that their confidential material is being shared over the Internet. People have called for his arrest and assassination. In December 2010, Assange was taken into custody in England on allegations of sexual assault in Sweden. As of April 2011, he still faced possible extradition to Sweden.

QUOTE

"Every organization rests upon a mountain of secrets." —*Julian Assange*

GLOSSARY

collateral
In terms of the US military, damage that is unintended.

encryption
Changing computer data into a secret code so it can be transmitted securely.

Guantanamo Bay
A prison facility located in Cuba and operated by the United States to hold detainees from the wars in Iraq and Afghanistan.

Interpol
A policing organization that coordinates international crime investigations.

mirror site
A Web site that is a copy of an existing site.

modem
A device or software that allows communication between computers.

nomadic
A lifestyle characterized by traveling from place to place without a permanent home.

Pentagon
The five-sided building near Washington DC that serves as headquarters of the US Department of Defense.

propaganda
Information conveyed in a biased way that is meant to sway public opinion.

public domain
> Documents or other media that are not copyrighted and therefore belong to the public.

scoop
> Information that is broadcast or printed by a news outlet before its rivals.

server
> Centralized computer hardware or software that manages a computer network.

subversive
> Undermining established authority.

transparency
> With regard to government practice, having information open to the public.

treason
> The crime of betraying one's country.

whistle-blower
> A person who informs authorities about an individual or an institution he or she thinks is involved in illegal activity.

wiki
> A Web site that can be added to and changed by any user.

ADDITIONAL RESOURCES

SELECTED BIBLIOGRAPHY

CBS News. "Julian Assange, The Man Behind WikiLeaks." *60 Minutes*. CBSNews.com, 31 Jan. 2011. Web. 3 Feb. 2011.

Gellman, Barton. "Person of the Year 2010: Julian Assange." *Time*. Time Inc., 15 Dec. 2010. Web. 3 Feb. 2011.

Greenberg, Andy. "An Interview with WikiLeaks' Julian Assange." *Forbes*. Forbes.com, 29 Nov. 2010. Web. 22 Mar. 2011.

Khatchadourian, Raffi. "No Secrets: Julian Assange's Mission for Total Transparency." *The New Yorker*. Condé Nast Digital, 7 Jun. 2010. Web. 22 Mar. 2011.

FURTHER READINGS

Doak, Robin S. *Conflicts in Iraq and Afghanistan*. Milwaukee: World Almanac Library, 2006. Print.

Halpin, Mikki. *It's Your World—If You Don't Like It, Change It: Activism for Teenagers*. New York: Simon Pulse, 2004. Print.

Lansford, Tom. *Political Activism*. Farmington Hills, MI: Greenhaven, 2007. Print.

Parks, Peggy G. *Computer Hacking*. Farmington Hills, MI: Lucent, 2008. Print.

Web Links

To learn more about Julian Assange, visit ABDO Publishing Company online at **www.abdopublishing.com**. Web sites about Julian Assange are featured on our Book Links page. These links are routinely monitored and updated to provide the most current information available.

Places to Visit

Computer History Museum
1401 N. Shoreline Blvd., Mountain View, CA 94043
650-810-1010
http://www.computerhistory.org
The Computer History Museum houses the world's largest collection of computer hardware, software, and other material related to the history of computing.

The Pentagon
Office of the Assistant Secretary of Defense for Public Affairs
1400 Defense Pentagon, Washington, DC 20301-1400
703-697-1776
http://pentagon.afis.osd.mil
The Pentagon serves as headquarters of the US Department of Defense, a virtual city unto itself where 23,000 military and civilian employees plan and execute US defense.

US Department of State
2201 C Street NW, Washington, DC 20520
202-647-4000
https://receptiontours.state.gov
The State Department is responsible for US international relations and implements US foreign policy and diplomacy.

SOURCE NOTES

Chapter 1. The Most Dangerous Man

1. Brian Boyd. "Robin Hood of Hacking." *Irish Times*. IrishTimes.com, 26 Jun. 2010. Web. 11 Jan. 2011.

2. Msnbc.com Staff. "US pilot seen firing on people in Iraq." *msnbc.com*. msnbc.com, 5 Apr. 2010. Web. 17 Jan. 2011.

3. "Wikileaks co-founder speaks about the leaked video of civilians killed in Iraq." *The Aryana Show*. Russian Television, 6 Apr. 2010. Web. 14 Jan. 2011.

4. "Profile: Julian Assange, the Man Behind WikiLeaks." *The Sunday Times*. Times Newspapers Ltd, 11 Apr. 2010. Web. 17 Jan. 2011.

5. "Wikileaks co-founder speaks about the leaked video of civilians killed in Iraq." *The Aryana Show*. Russian Television, 6 Apr. 2010. Web. 14 Jan. 2011.

6. WikiLeaks. "Donate." *WikiLeaks.org*. N.p., n.d. Web. 12 Jan. 2011.

7. "Big Brother is Watching: Wikileaks." *Churchill Security Limited*. Churchill Security Ltd, 2010. Web. 14. Apr. 2011.

Chapter 2. A Vagabond Boyhood in Australia

1. Raffi Khatchadourian. "No Secrets: Julian Assange's Mission for Total Transparency." *The New Yorker*. Condé Nast Digital, 7 Jun. 2010. Web. 13 Jan. 2011.

2. Ibid.

3. Andrew Strutton. "Rogue website author local lad." *Townsville Bulletin*. North Queensland Newspaper Company, 29 Jul. 2010. Web. 20 Jan. 2011.

4. "Julian Assange's mother recalls Magnetic." *Island News*. N.p., 7 Aug. 2010. Web. 20 Jan. 2011.

5. Kieran Campbell. "WikiLeaks founder a PC whiz: mum." *Sunshine Coast Daily*. APN Online, 5 Dec. 2010. Web. 24 Jan. 2011.

6. Lauren Wilson. "WikiLeaks Founder Julian Assange Was Hooked to Computer as a Boy." *The Australian*. News Limited, 15 Jan. 2011. Web. 14 Jan. 2011.

Chapter 3. Legal Battles

1. Raffi Khatchadourian. "No Secrets: Julian Assange's Mission for Total Transparency." *The New Yorker*. Condé Nast Digital, 7 Jun. 2010. Web. 13 Jan. 2011.

2. Ibid.

3. Andy Greenberg. "An Interview with WikiLeaks' Julian Assange." *Forbes*. Forbes.com, 29 Nov. 2010. Web. 24 Jan. 2011.

4. Lauren Wilson. "WikiLeaks Founder Julian Assange Was Hooked to Computer as a Boy." *The Australian*. News Limited, 15 Jan. 2011. Web. 14 Jan. 2011.

5. "Profile: Julian Assange, the Man Behind WikiLeaks." *The Sunday Times*. Times Newspapers Ltd, 11 Apr. 2010. Web. 17 Jan. 2011.

6. Lauren Wilson. "WikiLeaks Founder Julian Assange Was Hooked to Computer as a Boy." *The Australian*. News Limited, 15 Jan 2011. Web. 14 Jan 2011.

7. Raffi Khatchadourian. "No Secrets: Julian Assange's Mission for Total Transparency." *The New Yorker*. Condé Nast Digital, 7 Jun. 2010. Web. 13 Jan. 2011.

8. Andy Greenberg. "An Interview with WikiLeaks' Julian Assange." *Forbes*. Forbes.com, 29 Nov. 2010. Web. 24 Jan. 2011.

9. AFP. "Mother of Julian Assange fears for his safety." *The Swedish Wire*. Swedishwire.com, 2 Dec. 2010. Web. 19 Jan. 2011.

Chapter 4. WikiLeaks

1. Julian Assange. "State and Terrorist Conspiracies." *iq.org*. N.p., 10 Nov. 2006. Web. 25 Jan. 2011.

2. "Profile: Julian Assange, the Man Behind WikiLeaks." *The Sunday Times*. Times Newspapers Ltd, 11 Apr. 2010. Web. 17 Jan. 2011.

3. Raffi Khatchadourian. "No Secrets: Julian Assange's Mission for Total Transparency." *The New Yorker*. Condé Nast Digital, 7 Jun. 2010. Web. 25 Jan 2011.

4. Carole Cadwalladr. "Julian Assange, monk of the online age who thrives on intellectual battle." *Guardian*. Guardian News and Media Limited, 1 Aug. 2010. Web. 25 Jan. 2011.

5. WikiLeaks. *WikiLeaks*, n.d. Web. 26 Jan. 2011.

6. Jonathan D. Glater. "Judge Reverses His Order Disabling Web Site." *New York Times*. New York Times, 1 Mar. 2008. Web. 26 Jan. 2011.

7. CBS News. "Julian Assange, The Man Behind WikiLeaks." *60 Minutes*. CBSNews.com, 31 Jan. 2011. Web. 3 Feb. 2011.

8. "Profile: Julian Assange, the Man Behind WikiLeaks." *The Sunday Times*. Times Newspapers Ltd, 11 Apr. 2010. Web. 17 Jan. 2011.

Chapter 5. Afghan War Logs

1. CBS News. "Julian Assange, The Man Behind WikiLeaks." *60 Minutes*. CBSNews.com, 31 Jan. 2011. Web. 3 Feb. 2011.

2. "Bradley Manning, in his own words: 'This belongs in the public domain.'" *Guardian.co.uk*. Guardian News and Media Limited, 1 Dec. 2010. Web. 14 Apr. 2011.

3. Kevin Poulsen and Kim Zetter. "U.S. Intelligence Analyst Arrested in Wikileaks Video Probe." *Wired*. Condé Nast Digital, 6 Jun. 2010. Web. 27 Jan. 2011.

4. Ibid.

5. "Other views on WikiLeaks: 'We went through extra steps.'" *USA Today*. USA Today, 27 Oct. 2010. Web. 14 Apr. 2011.

6. Philip Shenon. "Pentagon Manhunt." *The Daily Beast*. The Newsweek/ Daily Beast Company, 10 Jun. 2010. Web. 27 Jan. 2011.

7. Julian Assange. "The truth will always win." *The Australian*. News Limited, 7 Dec. 2010. Web. 24 Jan. 2011.

8. Nick Davies and David Leigh. "Afghanistan war logs: Massive leak of secret files exposes truth of occupation." *Guardian*. Guardian News and Media Limited, 25 Jul. 2010. Web. 27 Jan. 2011.

Source Notes Continued

9. "Guardian Editor on Coverage of Afghan War Logs: European Audience 'Troubled More . . . by the Toll this War is Taking on Innocent People.'" _Democracy Now_. N.p., 27 Jul. 2010. Web. 28 Jan. 2011.

10. Julian Assange. "The truth will always win." _The Australian_. News Limited, 7 Dec. 2010. Web. 24 Jan. 2011.

11. "WikiLeaks Founder Says 'Evidence of War Crimes' in Afghan War Logs, White House Downplays Leak, Claiming 'No Broad New Revelations.'" _Democracy Now_. N.p., 27 Jul. 2010. Web. 28 Jan. 2011.

12. Carole Cadwalladr. "Julian Assange, monk of the online age who thrives on intellectual battle." _Guardian_. Guardian News and Media Limited, 1 Aug. 2010. Web. 25 Jan. 2011.

Chapter 6. Iraq War Logs

1. Robert Winnett. "Wikileaks Afghanistan: FBI called in to hunt those responsible." _The Telegraph_. Telegraph Media Group Limited, 29 Jul. 2010. Web. 31 Jan. 2011.

2. "Julian Assange Responds to Increasing US Government Attacks on WikiLeaks." _Democracy Now_. N.p., 3 Aug. 2010. Web. 31 Jan. 2011.

3. David Leigh. "WikiLeaks founder Julian Assange in web furore over Swedish rape claim." _Guardian_. Guardian News and Media Limited, 22 Aug. 2010. 31 Web. Jan. 2011.

4. Ibid.

5. "Wikileaks chief fights for job and reputation." _China Daily_. China Daily Information Company, 19 Sept. 2010. Web. 14 Apr. 2011.

6. "Publication of Afghan informant details worth the risk: WikiLeaks founder Julian Assange." _The Australian_. News Limited, 29 Jul. 2010. Web. 31 Jan. 2011.

7. Kevin Poulsen and Kim Zetter. "Unpublished Iraq War Logs Trigger Internal WikiLeaks Revolt." _Wired_. Condé Nast Digital, 27 Sep. 2010 Web. 27 Jan. 2011.

8. Isabelle Fraser. "The War on Secrets." _The Isis_. The Isis, 3 Dec. 2010. Web. 18 Jan. 2011.

Chapter 7. Cablegate

1. "Leaked U.S. Documents from WikiLeaks." _BBC News Blog_. BBC News Blog, 28 Nov. 2010. Web. 2 Feb. 2011.

2. Josh Sanburn. "Who Will Be Time's 2010 Person of the Year?" _Time_. Time Inc., 10 Nov. 2010. Web. 21 Jan. 2011.

3. Robert Mackey. "Reaction to Leak of U.S. Diplomatic Cables, Day 2." _New York Times_. The New York Times, 29 Nov. 2010. Web. 2 Feb. 2011.

4. Barton Gellman. "Person of the Year 2010: Julian Assange" _Time_. Time Inc., 15 Dec. 2010. Web. 3 Feb. 2011.

5. Alex Moore. "Julian Assange: Life is Hard in a World Without Hippies." _Death and Taxes_. N.p., 23 Oct. 2010. Web. 1 Feb. 2011.

6. Jim Sciutto, Russell Goldman, and Lee Ferran. "Julian Assange Says Document Dump Targets 'Lying, Corrupt and Murderous Leadership.'" *abcnews.com*. ABC News Internet Ventures, 29 Nov. 2010. Web. 2 Feb. 2011.

7. Ibid.

8. Kevin Poulsen and Kim Zetter. "U.S. Intelligence Analyst Arrested in Wikileaks Video Probe." *Wired*. Condé Nast Digital, 6 Jun. 2010. Web. 27 Jan. 2011.

Chapter 8. Hiding and Arrest

1. Carolyn Presutti. "Wikileaks Publisher Julian Assange Released from Jail." *Voice of America*. VOANews, 16 Dec. 2010. Web. 3 Feb. 2011.

2. John F. Burns. "WikiLeaks Founder on the Run, Trailed by Notoriety." *New York Times*. New York Times, 23 Oct. 2010. Web. 14 Jan. 2011.

3. Owen Bowcott. "Julian Assange to be questioned by British police." *Guardian*. Guardian News and Media Limited, 7 Dec. 2010. Web. 3 Feb. 2011.

4. Andy Barr. "Ron Paul stands up for Julian Assange." *Politico*. Capitol News Company, 3 Dec. 2010. Web. 3 Feb. 2011.

5. Carolyn Presutti. "Wikileaks Publisher Julian Assange Released from Jail." *Voice of America*. VOANews, 16 Dec. 2010. Web. 3 Feb. 2011.

6. Peter Grier. "WikiLeak's Julian Assange: Does Sarah Palin think CIA should 'neutralize' him?" *The Christian Science Monitor*. The Christian Science Monitor, 30 Nov. 2010. Web. 18 Jan. 2011.

7. Ibid.

8. "Pentagon Whistleblower Daniel Ellsberg: Julian Assange is Not a Terrorist." *Democracy Now*. N.p., 31 Dec. 2010. Web. 13 Jan. 2011.

Chapter 9. WikiLeaks Revolution

1. Andy Greenberg. "WikiLeak's Julian Assange wants to spill your corporate secrets." *Forbes*. Forbes.com, 12 Dec. 2010. Web. 18 Jan. 2011.

2. Ibid.

3. Andy Greenberg. "An Interview with WikiLeaks' Julian Assange." *Forbes*. Forbes.com, 29 Nov. 2010. Web. 24 Jan. 2011.

4. Ibid.

5. Kieran Campbell. "WikiLeaks founder a PC whiz: mum." *Sunshine Coast Daily*. APN Online, 5 Dec. 2010. Web. 24 Jan. 2011.

6. "WikiLeaks: Daniel Assange calls for father to be treated fairly." *The Telegraph*. Telegraph Media Group Limited, 8 Dec. 2010. Web. 24 Jan. 2011.

7. "Brett Assange: 'He was a very sharp kid.'" *CNN Seven Network*. Cable News Network, 9 Dec. 2010. Web. 24 Jan. 2011.

8. Daniel Schorn. "Julian Assange, The Man Behind WikiLeaks." *60 Minutes*. CBSNews.com, 31 Jan. 2011. Web. 3 Feb. 2011.

INDEX

ABOUT THE AUTHOR

Melissa Higgins writes fiction and nonfiction for children and
teens. She has a master's degree in counseling from Arizona State
University.

PHOTO CREDITS

Dan Kitwood/Getty Images, cover, 3; Bertil Ericson/SCANPIX/
AP Images, 6, 97 (bottom); Iain Masterton/Alamy, 8; AHMAD
AL-RUBAYE/AFP/Getty Images, 15; Walter Bibikow/Getty Images,
16, 96 ; Max Nash/AP Images, 23; Aaron Harris/Canadian Press/
AP Images, 24, 97 (top); CulturalEyes-DH/Alamy, 33; Salvatore
Di Nolfi/AP Images, 34; Mohamed Sheikh Nor/AP Images, 38;
Fabrice Coffrini/AFP/Getty Images, 45; Martial Trezzini/AP
Images, 46; AP Images, 49, 98 (top); Peter Macdiarmid/Getty
Images, 57; Maya Alleruzzo/AP Images, 58; John Stillwell/Press
Association/AP Images, 67, 99; Thomas Coex/AFP/Getty Images,
68; Sang Tan/AP Images, 72; Jewel Samad/AFP/Getty Images, 77;
Lennart Preiss/AP Images, 78; Stefan Rousseau/AP Images, 81;
Chris Radburn/AP Images, 85, 98 (bottom); Michael Sohn/AP
Images, 86; Ben Stansall/AFP/Getty Images, 91; Carl Court/AFP/
Getty Images, 95